Picture book of Britain in colour

Picture book of
Britain
in colour

Hamlyn
London · New York · Sydney · Toronto

Half-title page:
this stretch of coast in County
Antrim, Northern Ireland, affords a
spectacular view of the White Rocks
and, beyond, of Dunluce Castle.
The ruined tower and gables are
separated from the mainland by a
chasm, and one particularly eerie
aspect of the castle's history was
the storm in 1639 which carried off
part of the servants' quarters, and
the incumbent servants, and swept
them into the sea.

Title page:
the spire of Holy Trinity Church,
Stratford-on-Avon, rising above the
trees and the river is one of the
famous sights of Britain, and this
scene indicates how the town has
retained its essentially rural
atmosphere despite the fact that
some 300,000 people come every
year to visit the memorials to its
celebrated son.

Title verso:
five of Henry VIII's wives lived in
the noble proportions of Hampton
Court, the palace which Cardinal
Wolsey began and which remained
a residence of kings until the
ascension of George III, who
disliked it. Since then it has been
a much-visited museum; the picture
gallery is particularly celebrated.

Contents page:
Loweswater in the Lake District,
lesser known perhaps than many
places in that region but here
proving that it is no less worthy of
attention, wearing its summer
colours like a peacock.

Published by
The Hamlyn Publishing Group Limited
London · New York · Sydney · Toronto
Astronaut House, Feltham, Middlesex,
England

ISBN 0 600 36905 6
Depósito legal B. 41113-1973
Printer, industria gráfica sa
Tuset, 19 Barcelona
San Vicente dels Horts 1973
Printed in Spain

Contents

Seashore

Rude, cruel, wine-dark, tempest-tossed . . .
the poets' epithets for the sea have crashed or
danced about our ears for centuries, and for
those bred on these shores it must rank among
the most favoured founts of inspiration.
Not surprisingly. There must be few land
masses in the world that have a coastline
whose beauty and variety can equal that of
Britain's, and even fewer for whom the coastline
is so eminently accessible. We fortunates who
inhabit these islands may easily forget that
across the face of the great continents there
are millions of people for whom the sight and
sound and smell of the sea are untasted joys,
millions more for whom the one experience
of it has been a scruffy over-populated beach
or an oil-scarred port. Yet here there is nowhere
that is not within less than a day's drive of

the great salt water. And the choice is infinite —
beaches, bays, rocks, cliffs, coves, harbours,
shingle, sand; gulches echoing with the suck
and pull of the tides; pebbled beaches bleached
smooth by salt and sun, where the high-water
mark leaves slivers of seaweed draped across
the stones; the great jagged seascapes of
Cornwall where the western seas gnaw at the
rock-face; those crumbling and sometimes
cheese-yellow southern cliffs of chalk with
their overgrown grassy tops; the wide curved
sweep of Pembrokeshire bays that end in a
tapering headland, and in whose waters may
still be seen the rare pleasure of a family of
seals; the crude saw-tooth'd outline of the
Western Scottish coast with its wild sea-lochs
and its haphazard collection of oddly-named
islands; the North Sea beaches, long and

npty, packed by dunes and tufted grass,
nipped clean by the grey fury of the wind;
e flat silver-streaked estuaries of the
uth-east where the sea birds flight in at
sk over the thin margin of land and pierce
e darkness with their demonic cries; the
hing-boat-bobbing quays and harbours
 the holiday havens, the beaches where
ice ignorant armies clashed by night and
here now the summer bodies fight daily for a
vel stretch of sand.
norant armies or not, once upon a time all
sitors to Britain had to come by sea —
aesar waded through the shallows off the
ent coast, William marched stoutly up that
ussex beach, the Norsemen slid their
eat-prowed vessels across the sands at varying
oints north and east. Nowadays, more often

than not, the visitor is winged in across the
skies and may see no more of the coast than
a far-off creaminess at the land's edge or a
necklace of lights briefly twinkling in some
holiday resort. This chapter comes first in this
book to redress the balance. Something of
tradition, some demand for historical perspective,
requires that the importance and the splendours
of these seashores be acknowledged first of all.

Far left: the coast of Essex with its
creeks and inlets and long-winding
estuaries still has an air of
surreptitious invasion. The winkle
boats unloading their catch onto
the mudflats near Burnham-on-
Crouch are plying honourable trade,
but these mazy waters that stretch
so far inland have seen in their time
the stealth of less legal invaders,
those who have come by night and
disturbed none but the teeming
wildlife of this area.
Left: the fishing boats in the harbour
at Wick, Caithness, are sturdy
craft, built to ride out the
inhospitality of the North Sea in
search of herring, for which this
town is a centre. A royal burgh, it
also boasts a ruined castle to the
south, one of many in this
embattled corner of the land.
Previous page: fine unmolested
sands near Durness, Sutherland, on
the most northerly coastline of
Britain — virtually unmolested, in
fact, since the Norsemen arrived
here in 1034, stayed for two
centuries, and left without evidence
of their occupation.

Had lighthouses existed in 1588 the Spanish Armada would no doubt have been saved a few galleons as they fled round the coast of Britain. Not even the extremities of the land were lit then. *Far left:* the northernmost point of the mainland is not John O'Groats but Dunnet Head, whose lighthouse rakes the Pentland Firth separating it from Hoy and the Orkney Islands, a stretch of water notorious for its treachery. Some 900 miles to the south and west is the Longships Lighthouse off Land's End (*centre*), which some still think of as the last stepping-stone before the Great Unknown.

Left: Burnham-on-Sea, Somerset, has two lighthouses, one conventional, the other this quaint and unforbidding watchtower on the sands.

Below: the stretch of coast round Portland Bill, Dorset, is well-known for the Pulpit Rock, the Chesil Bank, and not least for the handsome lighthouse on the Portland Bill promontory.

Left: the coastline at opposite ends of England. Embleton Bay with its broad sweep of sand and fringe of coarse grass is typical of the Northumberland seashore, perhaps the most romantic part of the country for those whose taste inclines to knights and castles and medieval warrings.
Dunstanburgh Castle, in the distance, is one of many such that stand crumbling in this northernmost English county; built in the 14th century and decaying since the 16th, it still affords a magnificent spectacle, and on days of bleak weather when the North Sea wind touches you like cold steel it is difficult not to feel the presence of ghosts from those bloody Border wars.
Above: Brixham Harbour in Devon, on the other hand, with its brightly painted trawlers could not present a cosier or more welcoming picture. William of Orange was no doubt glad of this when he landed here in 1688 to claim the Stuart throne, and a statue on the quay commemorates this fact. Sir Francis Drake, too, dropped anchor here with a captured Spanish galleon from the Armada, but less well-known perhaps is that it was within sight of this port that Napoleon embarked in *HMS Northumberland*, outward bound for his last exile on St Helena. Today Brixham remains resolutely sea-minded — the trawlers share the harbour with the pleasurecraft of holidaymakers, and the cries of the gulls still manage to outweigh the invading roar of traffic.

St Ives, Cornwall (*above*) has
appealed to a diversity of charac[
all through its history, from the
lady saint from Ireland who gave
her name to the town, to Perkin
Warbeck who landed here to beg[
his pursuit of Henry VII's throne.
A little further west down the no[
Cornish coast the sea-borne
traveller may meet with a more
rough-hewn spectacle – the
Botallack tin mine (*right*), near
St Just-in-Penwith. Abandoned
now to the Atlantic's battering, it
is no more than a relic of Cornw[
busiest industrial period. Its
appearance is deceptive, howeve[
for the shaft descends over a
thousand feet under the rock and
far out under the sea.
Left: White Park Bay in County
Antrim, Northern Ireland, and wh[
could be more natural just aroun[
the headland from such a crazy
phenomenon as the Giant's
Causeway than that horses, not
people, should inhabit the beach

The music-hall tradition is not dead in Britain. In the steep and cobbled streets of Clovelly, Devon (*right*), you can apparently still see the rolling gait of a fisherman on his way back down to the sea. And Blackpool (*above*), famous, lovely Blackpool, 'queen of the resorts', has always featured, with affection, in the songs and jokes of the music-hall. This view, taken from the top of the celebrated Tower on a stormy evening, owes nothing to the equally celebrated illuminations which attract so many visitors to the town. But it shows another striking feature – the seafront – which extends for seven miles, crammed with every possible attraction that a holidaymaker could want. Even the more sedate members of the political conferences held here must find it hard not to be a little diverted by its raffish charms. Let it not be thought, either, that Clovelly, or the fisherman, if fisherman he be, are mocked. This village, tucked into the wide sweep of Bideford Bay, and one of the most beautiful in Devon, is known for the precipitousness of its streets, the descent of which require a rare balance.

A huddle of houses, a few slight boats, and the enclave of a harbour, walled against the sea. The coast of Britain has many such communities, defiant and self-protective in the winter, swollen with visitors in the summer. For all the upheaval that the latter causes the character of these places remains unaltered. St Abbs, Berwickshire (*far left, top*), in the Border country of Scotland, preserves a distilled calm beneath the 300 ft cliffs that well up behind it. It has long known how to take care of itself — those same cliffs are riddled with smugglers' caves. In Cornwall, too, from which the other two pictures come, there is a streak of canny resilience, part perhaps of the Celtic inheritance. Mousehole (*far left, bottom*) is well-named as it lies hidden behind an almost circular harbour wall, and Port Isaac (*left*), on the north coast of that county, looks virtually impregnable with its narrow sea-entrance and its guardian hills. To add to this impression of fortification, nearby are the remains of Castle Dameliock, the 'Castle Terrible' of the *Morte d'Arthur*.

London

Familiar friends in high places, enjoying a cleaner London air these days since the problems of pollution began to be tackled and America's idea of England's capital, as expressed in those fog-bound songs and smog-ridden movies, was banished. Trafalgar Square's Nelson (*below*), Piccadilly's Eros (*right*), the Old Bailey's Statue of Justice (*far right*), symbolic all three of some kind of conquest, now gleam with a new lustre on sunny days.
Previous page: it isn't just brilliant weather that commands the view. From London's newest pinnacle, the top of the GPO Tower, the va[st] expanse of the city lies carpeted beneath, and for those who like t[o] circulate while eating, the restaurant revolves, completing th[e] circle every thirty minutes.

In practice, of course, all roads, rail-tracks, flight-paths and shipping-lanes lead to London, directly or indirectly. The visitor to Britain is dumped in the great metropolis before he has scarcely had time to reckon the currency or learn the rudiments of the language from simpler, friendlier folk in the country. Not that the natives of the capital are unfriendly — far from it, they exude that spry cheerfulness which greets all occurrences, civil or uncivil, with a quick volley of humour — but London is predominantly populated by people who are themselves visitors, a myriad of flat-dwellers struggling to grab their chance, involved only in the preoccupations of their own minds and bodies as they plough backwards and forwards between office desks and rented quarters. These people may not know how to show off London at its best to the stranger.

It depends where he wants to begin. According to age, habit or inclination the choice may lie between the traditional, the commercial or the contemporary. The first of these will tackle the monuments to King and Country, God and Justice, and on a fine day these can afford an appropriate grandeur of spectacle for the seeker of history, can elicit admiration or wry smiles from the student of architecture as he takes in the parks with their respective statuary (most remarkable of which, the Albert Memorial), the river with its respective palaces (here embracing the outer reaches of London by including Windsor, Greenwich and Hampton Court), courts of justice, seats of government, victorious warriors in stone, marble, bronze or perched remotely on a column, Tower Bridge,

Marble Arch, Hyde Park Corner, the freedom of the Mall on days when no traffic is allowed to interrupt that splendid walk, the chiming bells of the City churches on a Sunday when that square mile is emptied like a honeycomb of its bowler-hatted worker-bees. Curiously, those seeking the more contemporary pleasures of the capital gather, at the beginning of their great adventure, beneath Eros, one of the most traditional statues. From there they branch out, in spirit at least, to the caverns and studios where fashion and music and literature spawn like multi-coloured mushrooms, which have helped to give to London once again the reputation of a great creative centre. On its streets, from the King's Road to Notting Hill Gate, the visitor may see and hear the barometers of taste fluctuate with bewildering speed.

Between these walks of life, and spanning the gap like a bridge, is commercial London. Here the visitor may indulge in the traditional airs-and-graces of a shopping expedition (for that is what it must be) through the courteous West End jungle, or he may venture to those areas where a good buy usually involves quick-wittedness and a ready understanding of the vernacular, the street markets that are full of surprises.

The past and present Palaces of London, only one of which is occupied by royalty today. Buckingham Palace (*left*), seen from the Mall on the day of the Trooping the Colour ceremony, was purchased from the Duke of Buckingham by George III, rebuilt by George IV, disliked by William IV, and finally occupied by Victoria, for the first time in the capacity of principal royal residence, though it was not until George V that the present facade was added. The Palace of Westminster (*below*) ranks as a palace, being in the charge of the Lord Great Chamberlain, but of its original features only the Great Hall still stands. At Greenwich (*bottom*) the grandiose buildings that represent the Royal Naval College were begun in the image of a palace for Charles II, to succeed the 15th-century Palace of Placentia, so beloved of Tudor sovereigns, which had stood here before, and in which Henry VIII was born and Edward VI died.

The Collegiate Church of St Peter in Westminster, commonly known as Westminster Abbey, probably has more popular history accumulated beneath its splendid roof than any building in the British Isles. Given that every English sovereign, bar two, since Harold has been crowned here and a generous proportion of that number buried, together with poets, soldiers, sailors, statesmen, to each of whom a plinth or slab or altar-tomb, the visitor has a millennium of history to digest before he can in good conscience return to the light of day. Many indeed become so devoted to these studies that they forget to look at the building itself, which is their loss because some of its features beggar all description. Among them is the stupendous grandeur of the nave, the highest Gothic example in England, here offset by the wreaths beneath it, round the tomb of the Unknown Warrior.

PHONE - ROYAL 6516
CANARY ISLANDS
LONDON
NAVIERA AZNAR S.A.
REGULAR CARGO AND
PASSENGER SERVICE
M/V MONTE ULIA
M/V MONTE URQUIOLA

Goods inward and goods outward.
As in most capital cities the
indigenous population of London
seem to be thriving noisy traders,
whether it be the well-heeled
backslappers of a city pub, the men
behind the transactions that see
great cargoes shipped and docked
in the shadow of Tower Bridge,
the early morning wheelers and
dealers of fish beneath the
Monument at Billingsgate, or the
stall-holders of Portobello Road,
purveying trinkets for the hoarder
and charms to catch the acquisitive
eye.

Fortress, prison, royal palace, the Tower of London's history is more writ in blood than parchment, and no matter how many tourists, cheerful and brightly-dressed, pass through its gates, nothing can expunge those ghosts that haunt its battlements, the presence of those so-called traitors, few of whom deserved the name, who looked, scratched or beat their last upon its walls. Among those murdered, executed, or here condemned to death have been Henry VI, the Duke of Clarence, Edward V, his brother Richard, Anne Boleyn, Thomas More, Catherine Howard, Lady Jane Grey, the Earl of Essex, Sir Walter Raleigh, the Earl of Strafford, Archbishop Laud, the Duke of Monmouth. Among the little pageantries continued today is the Ceremony of the Keys (*below*).

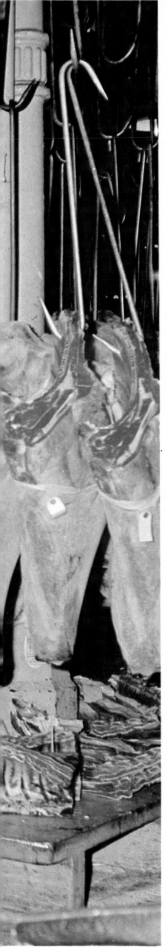

Once they executed traitors on the site of Smithfield Market, now they butcher meat; and now too they have executed Covent Garden, banished it south of the river to Vauxhall where it will lend its incomparable blend of crushed fruit and root crops, delicately touched with the scent of flowers, to the Thameside air. Covent Garden, undoubtedly one of the most attractive and best-loved areas of London, will miss its market sorely, though it may mean easier passage when the confusion of baskets and crates has been lifted. For compensation, turn to Smithfield in the early morning and watch the buyers from the grand hotels prod and argue over the quality of the fillet.

Normally you would only be
privileged to such a view of Hyde
Park Corner from some high perch
in St George's Hospital, and
certainly, at most hours of the day,
any attempt to enjoy the scenery
while circling in the maelstrom of
traffic invites a visit to St George's.
But here, for once, the sun shines,
the traffic is light, the view
stretches clear down Piccadilly, and
a string of London buses parade
dutifully for the camera, nose-to-tail
like circus ponies. Until the last
century this was the very outskirts
of London – from here westwards
it was countryside, and for those
who may think the rural atmosphere
has vanished for ever let them be
reassured that behind the doorway
in the south side of Decimus
Burton's Wellington Arch, or
Constitution Hill Arch, is a quite
unbelievably small police-station.

Below left: London, neat, calm, sharp as a pin and well-organized as a Canaletto. Even the barges seem tidily moored. In the far distance St Paul's and its surrounding buildings rise up as if mint-new; and Scott's *Discovery*, equipped to take the seas and winds of that howling southern continent, seems curiously misplaced with its three masts standing up like matchsticks against the summer green of the Embankment.

Below: neatness and formality have been dispensed with in a jumble of signs and occupations, a street of changing names, a cheerful distribution of beers, and the informal gatherings of people in the midday sun. Above pub and telephone booth and office block rises the current high-priest of London's skyline, from whose summit this chapter was begun.

Countryside

For the exile returning from abroad, the green of these islands can strike the eye with an almost uncharitable fierceness. Here, the field beside Blea Tarn Farm (Wordsworth's 'one abode, no more') in the Lake District has that brilliant sheen of after-rain, though the above-mentioned poet decided in his time that its colour could be attributed to the hard work of the farmer – 'made green by husbandry of many thrifty years'.

Previous page: an even more variegated collection of greens on the Island of Skye, where the mists regularly sweep down over the peaks of the Cuillins and ensure that the land remains permanently lush. But when the mists lift and the sun breaks through, this island's beauty knows few equals.

he motorways cross the land, but the land is
ot dead yet. Let him who thinks the countryside
ill not surprise him with a fine excess venture
to it with all his prejudices bundled in a
napsack and he will see them spilled upon
e ground. Lancashire is all industrial towns,
e may say, Wales all coal-blackened valleys,
ast Anglia all marshy fens, and who shall say
hich will be the greater, his shame when he
scovers the untruth of these generalizations
his pleasure at the beauties he did not know
ere there? Small though the surface area of
ritain may be, the unearthing of its various
nd numberless charms is an age-long process,
quiring time, patience with public transport,
eferably the initial guidance of one who
nows the area, and the will to explore.
nlike many other parts of the world, to drive
ong the arterial roads of Britain does not, in
eneral, give a fair impression of the nature
the land. Too often the roads demean the
ndscape instead of becoming platforms for
s greater admiration. In other places, of course,
ey are simply not capable of dealing with the
olume of people who rightly wish to enjoy
at corner of the country, roads that have
ot been stretched or straightened since they
ere first converted from muddy
orse-and-carted lanes. In some respects, the
ilways can give a truer picture, if only
ecause they allow for leisurely inspection
the landscape.
hat will he wish to see, this man who
xplores? Mountains, snowy or craggy,
alleys floored by heather or corn, dales that
ope away towards hills that buffet the clouds,

trim and green Home Counties downs? Will
he take the low road that winds to King
Arthur's Cornwall, or the high road that snakes
across the northern border, up into Scotland,
there to seek out the emptiness of the glens,
the open stretches of brown turf-sprung
moorland where the shaggy sheep stand
broadside to the wind and the curlew's cry
sounds like melancholy incarnate? Will he cross
the Brecons and visit the great glories of Wales,
or go beyond to the untethered beauties of
the Irish countryside where the hedgerows
spill into the roads? Will his restless eye yearn
for the level calm of vast East Anglian pastures,
or will it search for the plump landscapes of
the Weald of Kent? Such are some of the
obvious choices; there are less obvious ones
which space and time do not allow to be made,
and here in this chapter we may only represent
a selection of both the well-known and the
less-known, beauties acknowledged by
generations of travellers and some hitherto
unconsidered trifles, those that require the
hungrier spirit for their discovery.

For those who weary of formality, be it of life or landscape, there is no finer cure than time spent in the Lake District. Its ruthless and untrammelled countryside revives like no known tonic, arousing in the walker (for that is what any visitor to this area must be), through the rarefied quality of its air, that perfect sense of combined hunger and tiredness which only physical well-being can provide. It may rain for a week, and the clouds may roll inhospitably low over the crags, but the awesomeness of the area will not be diminished. Of course, as the saying goes, on a clear day you can see for ever; witness the pines against the snow at Grisedale (*above*), the long grey road that ribbons away to infinity at the end of Honister Pass (*right*), and the immaculate combination of sun, water, hill and whitewashed houses at Watendlath (*far right*). This last hamlet, by the tarn of the same name, Sir Hugh Walpole used as the principal setting for *Judith Paris* in his 'Herries' saga.

ong the best-known and most
ressive crags of the Lake
trict, the Langdale Pikes seen
t) rising above Blea Tarn, and
huge scarred side, like some
rly war-torn elephant, of Great
le (*above*). Those 'lusty twins',
Langdale Pikes look
comparatively benign on this fine
autumn day; in brutish weather,
especially in the snow, they take
on a formidable aspect. By
European standards, of course, they
are mere pimples – Harrison Stickle,
the higher, is 2,401 ft and Pike
O'Stickle 2,323 ft but in largely
mountainless England they provide
a whiff of that particular excitement
associated with hills that touch
the clouds. Great Gable is some
500 ft higher at 2,949 ft – this view
is taken from its neighbour Lingmell
– but may still be conquered by
the unroped walker.

Windmills with sails intact are rare now; at one time the flat eastern counties of England, just across the North Sea from even flatter Holland, abounded with them, and they could also be seen gracing the skylines of Sussex Downs with their angular scarecrow arms. Some still operate, others are restored to do so, though more often than not the tower is modified to become a 'desirable residence'. The well-preserved specimen on the opposite page is Salvington Mill, near Worthing.

Below: Preston Mill in East Lothian, Scotland, dependant on this stream for its propulsion, has here a delightfully secluded and overgrown air. So, too, has the water in front of the handsome whitewashed farm (*right*) near Kirkbean, Kirkcudbrightshire, in the south-west Lowlands. But let those who may scorn the Solway Firth as being of intemperate climate look now upon this scene, almost Mediterranean in its assembled brilliance.

Eden Valley in the Pennines,
well-named with its patchwork of
rich broad acres beneath a fine
expanse of sky. But it has its
serpent too, a devil much embraced
by local superstition, the Helm
Wind. No imaginary creature this, it
sweeps in violent icy blasts down
across the dales, and in the spring
may blow for a fortnight without
respite. It is at this time of year that
you may see the farmers with their
eyes fixed on the cloud formations,
for it is a particular gathering of
clouds over the hills that signals
the approaching onslaught of the
Helm. And, for the farmers,
onslaught is the word — crops have
been swept away, fences blown
down, cows and sheep tumbled
down hills or buried in snow-drifts
on the fell-sides, and bunches of
hay have been seen careering
across the sky, hundreds of feet up,
like a squadron of witches.

e inner countryside that soothes,
alm of hurt minds'.

akespeare used the quotation
fferently but he was not to know
e shock of pleasure that today's
rassed city-dweller finds in such
reats—lanes unpolluted except by
e farm tractor, cold clear light
rough silver birch trees onto that
nse silence of ferns, the
arvellous oppression of a day of
summer when the hedgerows

invade the path and long grasses
reach out to be plucked and
chewed.

Not until some fine surprising day in March do you feel the weight of winter lifted from the back of the land. Then, though the frosts may yet return and the month go out like a roaring lion, you are entitled to acknowledge that the days of fires, and overcoats, and dankness in the lungs, are numbered. The sunlit beech trees bordering the ploughed field are here caught on such a day of spring.

The summer has its weight too (*right*), the days of heat when the cumulus builds up around the edge of the sky into towering castles of wool and the air is heavy like a blanket. Suddenly the storm breaks, and with the rain the earth and air shuffle off their deadness like a snake its skin.

A remarkable Gothic scene, snow in the gulleys and storm clouds above, the last burst of evening sunlight turning the landscape a rancid gold as if signalling its readiness for sacrifice to the elements. All that it lacks is the accompanying soundtrack of horses' hooves and rattling carriage, the heroine fleeing to her lover . . .

No such lunacy affects the sequestered intimacy of these spring saplings (*inset*); even the photograph seems an intrusion on the private world of some unseen *Wind in the Willows* character.

Housman wrote of the
[col]oured counties', and from Clee
[i]n Shropshire (*top left*) you do
[g]et that impression of the quilt of
[fields] laid before your feet.
[Awa]y to the west is the border with
[Wal]es, still echoing with the
[ski]rmishes that inflamed the

Marches, the feuds that severed
Saxon from Celt.
Such magnificent panoramas are
found but rarely in the south of
England, as indeed are hills that are
both reasonably high and readily
accessible, which probably explains
why both Box Hill and Leith Hill,

near Dorking in Surrey, attract
visitors like a magnet. The scarred
appearance of Box Hill (*below
left*) bears witness to the thousands
who have slithered, slipped, rolled
or tobogganed down its satisfying
slopes.
Below: A fine view across the

water, and a fine feed for the gulls,
as the plough turns over virgin earth
near Loch Dunvegan on the Isle of
Skye.

There is not much to be said about the Mountains of Mourne (*left below*) that hasn't been better sung. They do sweep down to the sea, and are by general consent the most beautiful range in Northern Ireland. Stretching from Newcastle to Newry, they produce a dozen peaks above 2,000 ft, the highest being Slieve Donard which overlooks Newcastle and from its summit possesses magnificent views clear across to the Isle of Man.

Below: looking up towards the Black Mountains from the market town of Crickhowell in the lovely valley of the Usk, Breconshire. Over the other side is the English border, and at Crickhowell are the ruins of a 13th-century castle, one of a long line of strongholds in the Usk lowlands. Romans, Normans, Saxons have tramped these hills on missions of unholy war against the Welsh.

Mountains, moors and glens of darker aspect, the face of war, the long red thread in the tribal memory. This last will never be lifted from the name of Glencoe (*far right, top*), the 'Glen of Weeping', chosen, you might think, deliberately for its mournful dramatic impact by Campbell of Glenlyon when he set out to massacre forty Macdonalds in their beds. The clouds, the mists, the towering walls of rock combine to preserve the melancholy of that time.

The Romans fought to preserve what they had conquered; with a kind of crazed defiance they built a wall, seventy-three miles of it, across the top of England (*right*) to ward off the Celts. We may be grateful for the greatest surviving monument of their occupation, but how they must have suffered, those centurions from the warm south manning these frozen ramparts on the Northumberland moors. For 250 years they garrisoned it, with nothing to enjoy except the view.

Below right: the forest of Mamlorn, Breadalbane, Perthshire, has not such an immediate place in the history books, but its setting has a theatrical beauty, especially at that time of winter when the Grampians are snow-capped.

ole from the Cotswolds and
the Welsh hills, and rising
ndidly above the broad valley
he River Severn, the Malvern
(left) run for nine miles along
border between Worcestershire
Herefordshire, attaining nearly
0 ft at the highest point, from
re the view stretches to embrace
teen counties, including the six
efields of Worcester,
kesbury, Evesham, Shrewsbury,
ehill and Mortimer's Cross.
w left: the White Horse of
tbury, one of the many White
ses cut in the chalky Wiltshire
arpment. This one, known to be
ncient, possibly Iron Age,
in was remodelled in the 18th

century; and today the picnickers,
with scant respect for history,
unfold their baskets in its grassy
eye.
Below: Symond's Yat, Herefordshire,
where the Wye River twists through
a gorge ('yat' means gate or pass).
Famous as a beauty spot, it too
commands spectacular views.

Monuments

'Half church of God, half castle 'gainst the Scot.' So Sir Walter Scott wrote of Durham, and the inscription may be read on the bridge beneath the towering Cathedral. Most of the great buildings of this land have their inscriptions or their epitaphs, have been instruments of history or dramatic props of literature, and monuments — with its dictionary definition of 'anything that preserves the memory of a person or an event, a building, pillar, tomb, tablet, statue etc; any structure, natural or artificial, considered as an object of beauty or of interest as a relic of the past; a notable or enduring example' — seems to be the noun appropriate to embrace the collective virtues of castles, cathedrals, country houses, abbeys, stone circles and so forth, which are here gathered in this chapter. Again some of

them have stones that seep familiar history, others have walls which were only stormed in feuds of a more regional nature. The castles of Britain are worthy of anyone's study, but the pity of it is that so many have been left to fall into disrepair, abandoned to mouldering ruins either when the owner-family was besieged and uprooted, or when economics dictated that they could no longer be supported, or maybe (fancifully) when their history became too ghastly for their continued habitation and only ravens could abide the battlements which rang with the ghostly shrieks of tortured kings, the torments of Richard, Edward, false fleeting perjur'd royalty. Country houses, on the other hand, tend to have more sedate histories, built to ennoble the landscape as well as the life-style of their occupiers and

such are frequently preserved together with
their huge well-cultivated gardens.

The visitor to Britain could do worse, if time
restricted him, than travel to each of the
cathedrals. In so doing he would see the cities
and, in between, criss-cross the countryside.
And no two cathedrals are alike — the experience
of being in the presence of great architecture
will each time produce a whole complex of
emotions, each time differing in intensity
according to the effect of that particular
building. Great echoing naves with vaulted
roofs, saints and soldiers flattened with hands
clasped above their tombs, windows that
sometimes seem created, as do the cathedrals
themselves, beyond the call of duty, faith,
mortal endeavour. The abbeys too have their
greatness, and not a little sadness. Usually

more inaccessible than the cathedrals, and
deliberately so, their lovely ruined arches seem
to mock today's pedestrian efforts at grandeur
in concrete. Finally, and not least, the visitor
may wish to see one of the many groups of
ancient stones that stand about the country —
genuine monuments to a distant and only
partially understood past.

No contrast could be more
pronounced than that between the
fiery sunset over Castle Stalker and
Loch Linnhe in Argyll (*previous
page*) and the late summer sun on
Christ Church Meadows, Oxford.
Castle Stalker, silhouetted on its
island rock like something out of a
fairy tale, was built by Duncan
Stewart of Appin in the reign of
James IV, subsequently lost to its
owner as the result of a wager, and
is now a ruin. Christ Church has

seen its share of eccentric bets, but
none that actually involved the
disposal of the buildings. Founded
by Cardinal Wolsey it houses the
Cathedral church of Oxford,
has numbered the creator of Alice
in Wonderland among its
academics and a succession of
Prime Ministers-to-be among its
pupils. One of its further claims to
fame, Wren's Tom Tower, may be
glimpsed on this skyline of spires,
between the Cathedral and the Hall.

two fortresses, strong both
inst invasion. Tantallon Castle
beyond, at the mouth of the
of Forth, the Bass Rock. The
er used to house a castle, at one
a grim prison for Covenanters,
it was destroyed in 1694.
tallon was the seat of the for-
-feuding Douglases, and
sted all attempts at capture
General Monk bombarded it
twelve days in 1651. The
ding has been in decay since
end of that century when the
glases sold it.

ow left: Bodiam Castle, Sussex,
the other hand, never ever
ered an attack and thus remains
almost perfectly preserved
mple of 14th-century castle
nitecture, standing out above its
en snow-covered moat like
ry child's idea of a medieval fort.

ow: for a thousand years the
zens of Edinburgh have been
e to see their castle from every
quarter of the town, rising a clear
450 ft above sea-level, the sheer
wall on one side scaled only thrice
in all that time. Capital castle in the
capital city of Scotland, it has lost
none of its imposing grandeur in
this belittling age.

Sunlight on broken columns; arches tall, squat, delicate, and ornate; immaculate silence save for the wind flicking through hollow windows and the sudden jabbering of birds who have made their nest in a cloistered corner. The Abbeys of Britain are mostly ruins now, a fact which for some enhances their virtues of contemplative quiet and points up the noble patterns of their architecture.

Above: Crowland Abbey, Lincolnshire, built in the 8th century, burnt three times and shaken once by earthquake, now has only the North aisle and the tower surviving and this is used as a parish church.

Above right: Cleeve Abbey, Somerset, a late 12th-century foundation for Cistercian monks, has an excellently preserved refectory (reconstructed in the 15th century) and generally well-preserved convent buildings but the church is in ruins.

Far right: Melrose Abbey, Roxburghshire, 12th-century Cistercian also, and once one of the richest abbeys in Scotland, is far more extensive than this picture indicates, and among its hidden treasures is the heart of Robert the Bruce, supposedly buried beneath the East window.

Right: fair Fountains Abbey in the West Riding of Yorkshire, founded 1132, burnt, rebuilt, sacked by Henry VIII, and now among the most beautiful ruins in the country, seemingly grown in stature since its roof was dismantled and its wealth scattered.

A Border bastion, Caerlaverock Castle, Dumfriesshire (*above*), crumbling in its moat. Built in 1290 (though later much altered and added to), it changed hands between English and Scots like a bad penny, finally capitulating to the Covenanters in 1640 and thereafter being left to the elements. It has passed into literature as the 'Ellangowan' of Scott's *Guy Mannering*.

Right: the tattered ramparts of Corfe. Uneasy have lain the heads that wore the Crown inside this Dorset castle. In 978 the young King Edward was murdered by his stepmother, Queen Elfrida, at the gate of the Saxon stronghold that preceded the present Norman buildings; it was a favourite royal residence of King John; and poor Edward II was incarcerated here before being dragged away to his hideous death in Berkeley Castle. Finally it was defended for King Charles by Lady Bankes, gallantly resisting the onslaught of 600 Parliamentary troops until by treachery they seized it and by gunpowder reduced it.

: Bath has given its name to
s, biscuits, chaps and chairs, it
been called the 'Florence of
land', and in its time the pens
Dickens, Sheridan, Smollett,
ckeray, Fielding, Fanny Burney
of course Jane Austen have
e their literary best for it.
nan legions and Regency bucks
e delighted in its charms and
npled its waters for their aches
pains.
contrast until recent years,
entry's fame rested principally
cloth, cycles, cars, the long
nd tresses of one Lady Godiva,
a magnificent Gothic cathedral.

The cities share a common
experience. Bath, in no way a target
for war, was nevertheless wantonly
bombed in 1942 and had to be
extensively rebuilt, while Coventry,
on the night of 14 November 1940,
suffered the most appalling blitz
ever experienced by a British city.
As a result a whole new city was
built in the ruins of the old,
becoming in the process a
landmark of urban redevelopment.
Crowning this is the new Cathedral,
rising above and alongside the
hollow shell of its razed predecessor
(*above*).

Monuments from the Neolithic age, when rough-hewn stones served as the instruments by which the gods were summoned or placated. Beneath the great snowy hump of Blencathra in Cumberland the worshippers gathered and revolved in the Castlerigg Stone Circle, sometimes called the Keswick Carles, a ring of 48 stones with a maximum diameter to it of more than 100 feet. Not so obvious or well-known as Stonehenge, which served a similar purpose, it was built with a true sense of theatre in a bowl of mountains and some say became Keats' 'dismal cirque of Druid stones upon a forlorn moor'. *Inset:* the Legananny Dolmen in County Down, Northern Ireland, probably a Neolithic burial-chamber. The structure breathes weight; only fervent dedication could have put that stone up there.

e of the stately temples that
grace this land, to man, God,
olie de grandeur. Blenheim
ace (*bottom left*) has probably
e of the last, donated by a
eful Queen Anne to John
rchill, 1st Duke of Marlborough,
his string of victories in the Low
ntries, especially the one from

which the vast mansion takes its
name. The unfinished masterpiece
of Vanbrugh, it also owes its
glories to many other distinguished
craftsmen, and it renewed its
prominence in the history books by
being the birthplace of Sir Winston
Churchill.
Montacute House, Somerset

(*above*) seems to have all that was
best of the Elizabethan age.
Generous without being vulgar,
formal without being severe, it is
worthy of long pilgrimage.
Above left: the longest cathedral in
Europe, majestic square-towered
Winchester has seen kings crowned
and buried, homage paid and

ecclesiastical decree proclaimed
over the centuries in which its
city has been sometime joint-capital
of the land and its college the
cradle of aspiring scholarship.

Villages and Country Towns

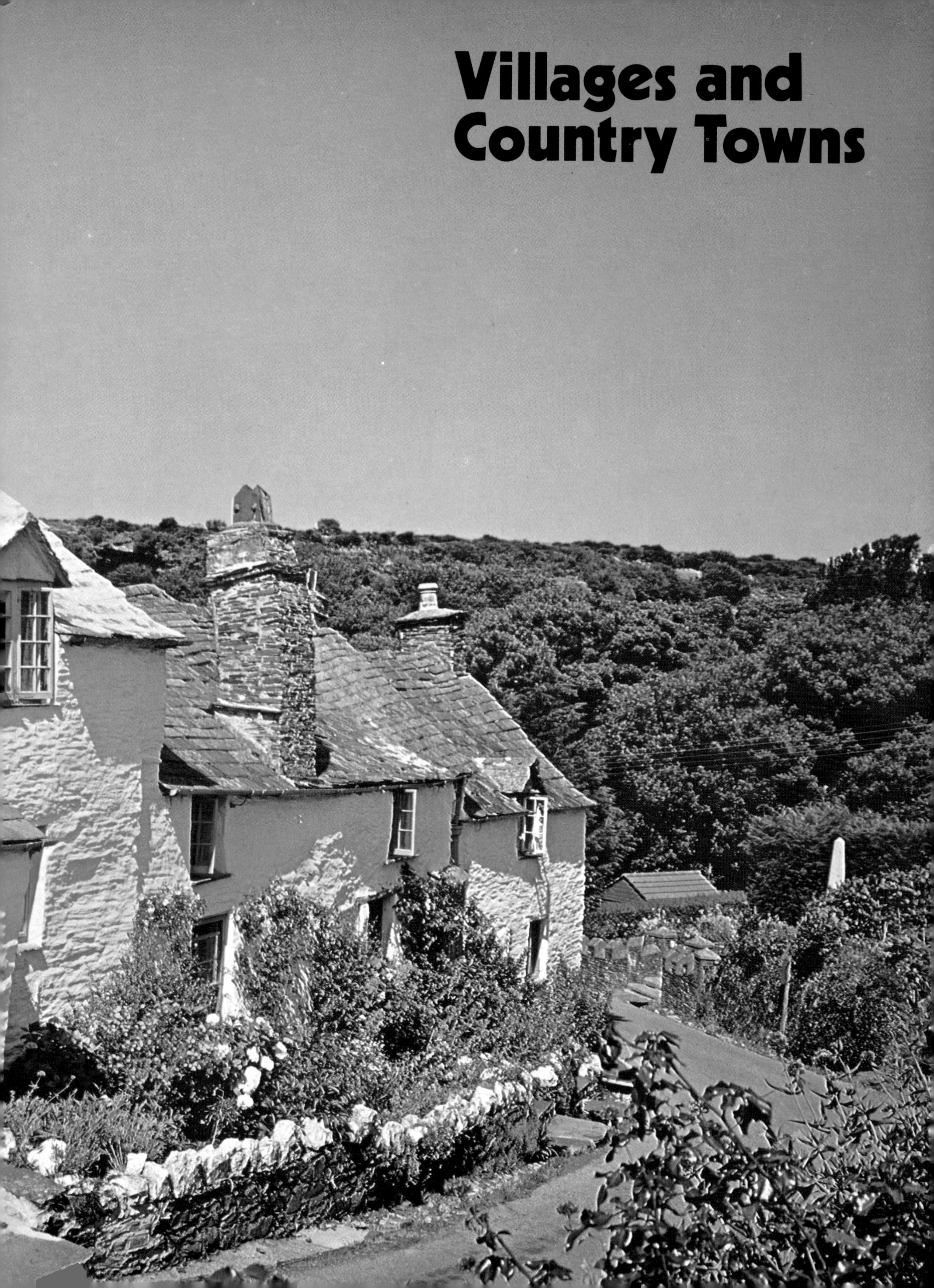

The villages and country towns of Britain,
the obvious beauties of the land, tend to be
the parts of the country that get spoiled in the
mind's eye by over-emphasis, by over-exposure
perhaps in the cinema travelogue or by the
too heavy tread of sentiment when thought
about in absence. Not that they are ever
spoiled in themselves — nothing short of nuclear
holocaust could do that, and it is perhaps
allowable for yet another voice to rise in praise
of their virtues. In this chapter, as indeed
throughout the book, the aim has been to
show the beautiful well-known with the
beautiful less-known, thereby affording a
broader vision of the countryside than a mere
assembly of picture postcards of famous views
could give. Those places that are familiar may
therefore be recognized with nostalgia by those
who have fleetingly visited them, and those
places that seem strange may hopefully either
be sought out or here acknowledged for their
charms. The choice was infinite — in every
county is a village that might be described as
'typical', in every village a scene that qualifies
as 'picturesque'. But what is 'typical'?
Cornish whitewashed houses on a steep road
that leads down to the sea, the warm brown
stone of Cotswold villages, rose-covered
cottages in Kent, tiny houses buried in the
Berkshire downs, the timber-frames of Suffolk,
the simple frontage of a row of Lakeland
dwellings — all these may be said to represent
the typical, but they are typical only of the
area they occupy and in which they are the
predominant feature, and that area can be very
small. To say they are typical of Britain is only

true insofar as they are not typical of France, or Norway, or Nigeria, because not found there. But within Britain to say one is typical is to say that all are, and many more for whom there is no room upon these pages.

One feature, though, which cannot escape notice and of which all visitors from abroad demand the experience — the English pub. To a few it is an over-rated institution, to most the very backbone of our country life, almost the local parliament, where reputations may be lost and won in an evening, yarns of immense length and increasing fiction spun for hours on end, boasts roared, threats taunted, quarrels mended and marriages sealed. 'I do but play with an imagined life,' wrote Browning, thinking of something else, but it is a fair bet that most Englishmen caught up in circumstances that separate them from home — war, foreign service, etc — do play at some time or another with an imagined life that centres round the bar, and the company, of a pub they have known in the country.

Like the country girl who becomes a film star overnight, and lives to regret her inability ever to return to the simple unfettered life, Castle Combe was swept to fame a few years back by being elected Prettiest Village in England and since then has struggled against the tide of invaders bent on confirming for themselves the rightness of this decision. The Hollywood moguls were among them, and it is a tribute to the enduring quality of this Wiltshire village that its charms remain untarnished.
Previous page: there are many Cornish villages that share the features of Boscastle, with its prominence of slate, the liberal laying-on of whitewash, the steep and narrow road that leads down to the sea. The nearby slate quarries of Delabole were in fact the original reason for Boscastle's existence, for its tiny harbour, overshadowed by precipitous cliffs, was built for the export of the slate.

ere are many, among them some
the greatest landscape painters
s country has known, who have
orn that the beauties of East
glia are without peer. Others,
ore used to the cosy proximity of
s, will argue that those endless
eeps of pancake-flat terrain, the
arshes, heaths and vast acreages
corn are an acquired taste. Never
quired unless attempted, and the
vitiate could do worse than aim
these two handsome
resentatives for a start. Norwich,
e capital of Norfolk, with castle,
thedral and, lately, university, has
the finest qualities of a provincial
y — activity, spaciousness,

generosity of spirit. Elm Hill (*left*),
with its cobbles and overhangs,
is among the best preserved of its
streets.
Suffolk's Lavenham (*above*)
thrives on preservation. A small
15th-century town that prospered
in the wool trade, fostered by those
huge East Anglian pastures, it has
determinedly kept what it has won,
in particular a predominance of
magnificent timber-framed houses.
Among them are the famous
Guildhall and Wool Hall, and several
which lean drunkenly one way or
another, chief of these being the
Crooked House pictured above.

ne of empty seats, but a few
ctators who still appreciate the
ce and subtleties of cricket, the
e the foolish say will die but
ch in fact has its roots buried
p in a country tradition—
erever a few level acres of grass
be found with a pub adjacent.
st would probably agree that the
nature of the game, its style
delicate sense of theatre, is
transmitted on summer
nings such as this when thirst
gthens with the shadows. They
ainly know it at Hambledon, as
did two hundred years ago
en the game is said to have been
n here, to which fact a memorial
ds witness on Broadhalfpenny
wn opposite the Bat and Ball

Discovered country to whose bourn the travellers return, the England that fills postcards and home-thoughts-from-abroad — ye olde inn, a jar of ale, thatched cottages swathed in the thick scarf of summer.

The small octagonal-shaped inn at St Albans (*top*), the Fighting Cocks, bears the legend that it is the oldest inhabited licensed house in England, while the Masons Arms (*above*) at Branscombe in South Devon can certainly lay claim to being one of the best examples of the genre.

In a delightful village, sheltered by hills on either side and reached by steep and twisting lanes, the pub is within a few minutes walk of the sea across the fields.

Right: Welford-on-Avon, Warwickshire, a view that summons up the charm and innocence of a long-lost childhood when all the world was summer.

'There live not three good men unhanged in England, and one of them is fat and grows old'. In fact Falstaff sits and grows old in stately bronze, holding court to the populace who visit his creator's native Stratford, the town which bore him, bred him, and finally, when the whirligig of time brought in its revenges, buried him. This last was done in Holy Trinity Church (*left*), beside the Avon, and the stone slab therein, together with the monuments of his life and the theatre which re-creates his plays, is one of the much-visited spots.

Above: another poet is connected with this place, Hawkshead in Lancashire near Coniston Water. Wordsworth attended the Grammar school and his name may be seen carved on one of the desks. He would no doubt have been aware of the 15th-century monastic court house pictured above, formerly the the property of Furness Abbey, and where once, in Falstaff's terms, the 'rusty curb of old father antic the law' could be heard and seen at work.

Three places all acknowledged for their fairness. Broadway (*above*) in Worcestershire is by popular consent the finest of the Cotswold villages, though popular consent may have, in the eyes of some, damaged its original appeal. Antique dealers and lordly motor-cars now provide opulent distraction in the broad main street, deserted here in this picture which shows to good effect the famous local Cotswold stone gleaming in a stormy light.

Bath (*below right*) has had its classical and 18th-century praises sung unstintingly, and perhaps these are most warmly felt today a population who can enjoy colonnaded walks where they ma shop away from traffic. And wha could be finer on a sunlit mornin than this prospect of the Abbey seen beyond baskets of flowers i full bloom?

Above right: the village is well-known even if the garden is not, but the garden ought to be, as an example of English horticultural pride and care. The garden is in the Huntingdonshire village of Hemingford Grey, which has a reputation both for being pretty and for containing what is possibly the oldest-inhabited house in England.

Below: these thatched cottages at Selworthy in Somerset are perhaps representative of what is best known and most photographed in the English countryside. Trim and unpretentious, they have been preserved through the generations by diligent re-applications of whitewash, and their ordered calm contrasts well with the haphazard profusion of trees behind them.

Such scenes are often to be found in Somerset—villages clutched in hollows while from above the view opens out across the valley to wooded hills beyond. From the churchyard just above these cottages, for instance, there is a magnificent prospect of distant Dunkery Beacon.

Right: Tintagel's history is long on legend, most of it connected with King Arthur, and visitors to this Cornish village rush to see the crumbling romantic ruins of its castle, which seems to ooze eventful past. In so doing it is easy to pass by the Old Post Office, pictured here, so called because it was a letter-receiving office in the second half of the 19th century but which in fact was built to the plan of a manor house in the 14th century, probably only two cent after the castle.

far as is known, no curfew
vails in Hutton-le-Hole in the
rth Riding of Yorkshire (*left*), nor
parently has the village been
serted on the grounds of fire,
nine or pestilence. Perhaps some
rained sense of Yorkshire thrift
s locked the inhabitants inside;
re probably it is the early hours
daylight and they sleep in honest
ds. The photographer is abroad
fore even the milk churns are
lected, aware of the photogenic
ssibilities of these interesting
nfigurations of white painted posts.

Above: Not a mouse stirs in
Pluckley either, in the Weald of
Kent, but an imaginative hand has
been at work converting this oast-
house and zebra-striped barn into
an eminently habitable home.

'The web of our life is of a mingled yarn, good and ill together.' In Shakespeare's time two of the places pictured here would have been important centres for that mingled yarn from which he drew his metaphor. Kersey (*far right*) built a sound prosperity on the Suffolk sheep, and gave its name to a cloth, while pride of place in Dunster, Somerset (*right*) still belongs to the Old Yarn Market, which dates from about 1600. Kersey, like Lavenham, is still unspoiled, and one of its incidental charms is the water-splash in the main street.

Below: '. . . good and ill together.' The clouds move on out over the Solway Firth, leaving puddles, mud, and watery light slanting across this attractive row of houses in Allonby, Cumberland.

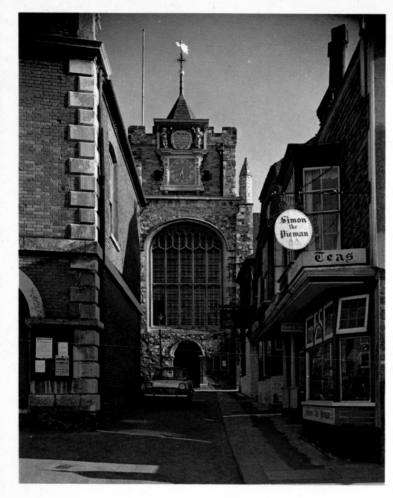

In many of the country towns of
Britain history can be dug up like
truffles, odd corners made more
interesting by the discovery of some
obliging curiosity. Both Rye (*above*)
in Sussex, and Cirencester (*right*)
in Gloucestershire can be rich
providers of such fare, having both
an extensive and noteworthy past.
Rye, sometime Cinque Port and
smuggling haunt, has been burned
down twice by the French, has seen
its surrounding countryside
submerged by the sea and has been
the home of Henry James.
Cirencester, *Corinium* to the Romans
and built by them to be the second
city of Britain, was destroyed by the
Saxons, invaded by the Normans
and subsequently restored to be a
thriving market town. Both towns
have, however, a curiosity in
common in these pictures.
Cirencester Parish Church is one of
the largest in England, and one of
the most beautiful examples of
Perpendicular, an unusual feature
being the elaborate three-storey
South porch. The Church of St
Mary in Rye, on the other hand,
has a clock which dates back to
the 16th century and is believed to
be the oldest in England still
functioning with its original
mechanism.

Inland Waters

How many would choose to live by one or other of these islands' waters if they were given the opportunity? This book began with the sea, which has been so much fortress, protector and benefactor; it ends with the inland waters of Britain which, for many, represent a haven and an ideal. Some worship the great rivers, Thames and Severn, Avon, Tees and Tyne, the 'smug and silver Trent', which trace like veins of mercury across the land; worship them for their traffic or their powers of commerce, for their strength which turns water mills or pumps electricity, but more likely, far inland, for their sweetness which carries them, the worshippers, along their watery backs in cabin cruiser, yacht, dinghy or canoe, from county to county taking days on end to accomplish what the aggressive motor-car will achieve in hours.

Others find Nirvana in the lakes, or lochs, or loughs, cradles of legend, of monsters (real or imagined?), giant puddles in the mountains from which they take their strength and depth. Here are the waters, brimming, bright and large, upon which the fisherman pushes out his boat and sits in undistracted solitude, far out in the silence while the white mists gather over his head like a wraith. And here, too, the sudden squalls blow up, pummelling the surface and pounding the waves like creamy fists through the reeds at the water's edge. The fisherman who seeks a louder setting will stand in the raging shallows of a river, casting for the fish that fight upstream against the current, listening to the thunder as the torrent splits its streams between the boulders, tumbles,

splits again, falls precipitate, and then regathers in a foaming cauldron at the base.

There are surely many who would like to live within sight and sound of water, even if it be only a wee burn rippling at the bottom of the garden. Nor is such a desire solely the prerogative of the romantic spirit. In this day and age, when the roar of traffic encroaches more and more upon the daily lives of thousands when the eardrums are penetrated by the most continuously unmusical sound that man has yet invented, it is no more than a sensible concern for physical and mental health which seeks to replace it with the rhythm of falling waters, no matter how furious or torrential. And for the eye, water, still or moving, and nearly always it is moving, however imperceptibly, is perhaps the most intensely watchable phenomenon of all It is to be hoped that this chapter will not create the impression of Britain as a land overflowing with rivers and lakes, a giant marsh of a country, for that would be untrue. These watery pictures are meant as an unspoken reassurance of the landscape's sanity, of what we may in troubled times consider as a longed-for refuge.

Ullswater, glimpsed (*below*) through trees on a windy autumn day, and (*above*) nailed by winter, flotsam tethered in jagged ice. This unusual effect was obtained by the lake freezing, then thawing, and the wind blowing the ice-floes to the shore, where they were gripped by another severe freeze.
Previous page: Derwentwater, crowned by the cold peak of Skiddaw and, with its withered reeds, looking like the setting for Keats' *La Belle Dame Sans Merci.* If you can bear the low temperatures a visit to the Lake District in the dead of winter can sometimes be more visually satisfying than at other times of the year.

ove: Buttermere and its
*ighbour Crummock Water seen
*om Fleetwith Pike—a sense of
*endid isolation, of magic lakes
*ewed from a dragon's lair as he
*ards the entrance to the pass. To
*me back to reality, these two
*es were once one, and it can be
*arly seen how they were cut in
*o, divided by the detritus brought
*wn by mountain streams.
*less it be thought the Lake
*strict is all barren crag and
*peopled pasture, let the eye
*st on the views of Grasmere and
*nmail Raise (*left*) from the fells

near Red Bank. Many will know
that Wordsworth, that master of
solitude, chose the community of
Grasmere as his home for ten years,
close by the nearly circular lake of
the same name with the island in
the middle, and it would be a stony
heart that did not think he chose
wisely.

Monuments to vaulting ambition, accomplished in different shapes and sizes. *Right:* the Clifton Suspension Bridge, one of the massive achievements (though not completed until after his death) of the great Isambard Kingdom Brunel, among other things engineer of the Great Western Railway and builder of the Great Western and Great Eastern Steamships. Begun in 1831, and incorporating suspension chains from Brunel's Hungerford Bridge, which was being demolished, it fills the sky 245 feet above the Avon Gorge. Older and more modest in proportions is the Clapper Bridge (*above*), built long ago out of slabs of stone. This particular one is near Great Asby in Westmorland, but they are most frequently found in Devon.

The soothing presence of water — in these frenetic times perhaps of more emotional benefit than practical. Under graceful Flemish-style bridges and flanked by lawns, the River Windrush runs parallel to the main street in the Cotswold village of Bourton-on-the-Water (*far left*). A further attraction here is a sizeable model of the village made out of the local stone.

Top left: a leisurely unsophisticated method of transporting a car across water via the Bann ferry at the entrance to Lough Neagh in Northern Ireland. This picture gives no indication that the lough is in fact by some considerable distance the largest lake in the British Isles. Eighteen miles long, eleven miles wide, ten rivers flow into it and five counties share its shores.

Below left: the sunlit steeple and the stacked houses of Ross-on-Wye above its curving river in that Herefordshire corner of England which numbers among the most cherished beauties of these islands.

Highland cattle stand in the shallows of Loch Etive (*above*) in Argyllshire, a great sea loch with a variety of wild scenery converging on its shores in its eighteen miles of length — woods, mountains, empty echoing glens, and at its mouth the Falls of Lora, the sea-rapids that cascade over a reef of rocks and whose music Ossian heard and made famous. These are now crossed by an impressive cantilever bridge.

Left: smaller but not less imposing, Llyn Gwynant in Caernarvonshire can be seen in its entirety, encircled by traditional Welsh scenery — acres of sheep pasture and the musical mountains that have sired all those poets with the dancing rain in their voices.

No savage splendour to these waters, only the continuous rubbing on the stone-cast of walls, the quick rippling of the surface as the breeze flicks it. The water that surrounds Ightham Mote (*far left*) is fresh from a spring, a natural moat to this handsome Kent manor house that was built in the 14th century, added to in the 15th, and has been occupied virtually without break since then.

Left: a ferry crosses the River Avon to this landing-stage at Fladbury in Worcestershire, though it is out of sight here, moored in the water-lilies along this bank and no doubt becalmed under the flat blade of indolent midsummer.

117

The much-loved and oft-frequented waters of East Anglia. *Left:* a convenient mooring on a bend of the River Bure at Coltishall on the Norfolk Broads, those waters that cover thousands of acres and which hordes of landlubbers take to navigating for their summer holidays, crazily tacking between the many attractive pubs that come down to the rivers' edge. The true nature of the Broads is best seen at those times of year when the wild life predominates, when in the reeds and marshes and shallows may be heard the frenzied orchestrations of a great variety of birds, some of them not commonly found elsewhere in England. *Above:* the Stour in Suffolk may not suffer the boating invasion of the Norfolk Broads but many thousands of eyes have feasted on it indirectly, through the works of Constable. He once said that he associated his 'careless boyhood with all that lies on the banks of the Stour; those scenes made me a painter'. Here is a stretch of that river, at Flatford, that must have seemed a paradise to a small boy with its secretive air.

Inset: the foaming River Swale at Richmond in the Yorkshire dales creates its own rough clothing of white samite.

all the places that claim
nection with the legends of
Arthur, the one that rings
st true is Dozmary Pool on
min Moor, Cornwall. Here, as
nyson gives guidance to
gination, Sir Bedivere 'came on
shining levels of the lake',
e untruthfully reported that he
rd only 'the long ripple washing
e reeds', and on the third time

clutch'd the sword
d strongly wheel'd and threw it.
he great brand
de lightnings in the splendour of
he moon

ere he dipt the surface, rose
n arm
thed in white samite, mystic,
wonderful,
d caught him by the hilt, and
randish'd him.
ee times, and drew him under in
he mere '

Not the great thunder of a Niagara or a Victoria, but a thin-lipped fury, a mare's tail lashing between rocks. Each of these falls has inspired a pen – George Borrow wrote of Pistyll Rhaeadr (*below*), on the borders of Denbighshire and Montgomeryshire, that he had never seen 'water falling so gracefully, so much like thin beautiful threads as here', and it is indeed the most magnificent waterfall in Wales.

Wordsworth was much enamoured of Aira Force (*right*), near Ullswater, and set *The Somnambulist* here.

The ribbon of rainbow falling across the fierce white waters certainly creates that kind of mystical effect of which he was so fond, as indeed does the exquisite misty stillness of Great Langdale Beck (*centre below*).

Man has made roads and runways and in the process more often than not has massacred the landscape, but where he has made rivers he has usually enhanced it. The dyke by Thurne Mill on the Norfolk Broads (*below left*) may have an austere straightness to it, and the heavy machinery at Laggan Locks (*below*) in Inverness-shire may seem a little cumbersome, but both lend favour to the eye when it sweeps the terrain looking for that strip of silver water, be it lake, river, canal, waterfall or duckpond, which so attracts the British for some deep-down reason, some subterfuge emotion buried far back in the race memory.

Away across the Firth of Forth
beneath the girders of its famous
railway bridge . . .

Acknowledgments

Peter Baker 49, 61, 111, 115

Barnabys Picture Library 39, 64 top, 72 top left, 90 top left

Roy Birks 124/125

G. Douglas Bolton 12, 20 top, 18, 58 top, 63 top, 66/67, 92/93, 108, 117, 118, 126

Vincent Brown 13 top, 31 top

Camera Press 86, 97

J. Allan Cash 16 bottom, 70 top, 75

Peter Cheze-Brown 17, 31 bottom, 120/121, 122 left

W. F. Davidson contents page, 12/13 top, 14, 20 bottom, 19, 42/43, 44 top and bottom, 45, 47, 48 top, 50, 51, 52, 53, 54, 55, 56 (inset), 56/57, 59, 62, 63 bottom, 72/73 bottom, 74, 76, 78, 84/85, 87, 92 left, 93 right, 95 top, 96, 100 top and bottom, 101, 104/5, 107 top and bottom, 109, 110, 112, 119, 120 (inset), 122 right, 123 right, 125 right

Eagle Photos Ltd 13

V. K. Guy 82/83, 91

The Hamlyn Group Photographic Library title verso, 16 top, 24/25, 27 top and bottom, 33, 38, 68/69, 71, 77, 80 top and bottom, 94, back cover top right

Jarrold and Sons Ltd front cover centre right, back cover top left and bottom

A. F. Kersting 28, 29, 58 bottom, 70 bottom, 81, 116

Keystone Press Agency Ltd 25 top left and right

David R. MacAlpine 48 bottom

Monitor Press Features Ltd 65, 95 bottom, 99

Picture Index Ltd 10, 88/89, 89 (inset)

Picturepoint Ltd front cover bottom, half title page, 22/23, 26, 32, 34, 35, 36/37, 60, 64 bottom, 102

Pix Photos Ltd title page, 113 bottom

Popperfotos front cover top left

Kenneth Scowen 90 bottom, 98, 114

Skyport fotos 79, 113 top

E. W. Tattersall 30

John Woolverton 8/9, 11, 15, 21, 40/41, 46, 72/73 top, 73, 103